*M*EDUSA'S *C*OUNTRY

Larissa Shmailo

MadHat Press
Asheville, North Carolina

MadHat Press
MadHat Incorporated
PO Box 8364, Asheville, NC 28814

Copyright © 2016 Larissa Shmailo
All rights reserved

The Library of Congress has assigned
this edition a Control Number of
2016915269

ISBN 978-1-941196-38-0 (paperback)

Cover art by Robert Hunt
Cover design by Marc Vincenz
Book design by MadHat Press

www.MadHat-Press.com

First Printing

Other Works by Larissa Shmailo

Poetry

#specialcharacters (Unlikely Books, 2014)

Fib Sequence (chapbook) (Argotist Ebooks, 2011)

In Paran (BlazeVOX [books], 2009)

A Cure for Suicide (chapbook) (Červená Barva Press, 2006)

Fiction

Patient Women, A Novel (BlazeVOX [books], 2015)

Translations

Victory over the Sun by Alexei Kruchenych (Červená Barva Press, 2014)

Bibliography of Bible Translations in the Languages of the Russian Federation, Other Countries in the Commonwealth of Independent States, and the Baltic States (American Bible Society, publication pending)

Recordings

Exorcism (SongCrew, 2009)

The No-Net World (SongCrew, 2006)

Dedicated to Ani, my uchitel', *with gratitude and love*

Table of Contents

I. ELUDED

To the Thanatos within Me	3
Gaia's Lunacy	6
Cardiac Ghazal	7
The More You Leave	8
Erasure, "The Lotus Eaters," *Ulysses*	9
Mean	10
Between Eclipses	11
Daddy's Elusive Love	12
My Vronsky	13
Sunken Virgin	14
The Searchers	15

II. DELUDED

My Dead	19
He Called Me "Fat"	20
Heart Murmur	21
The Trick Wants to Go to Plato's	22
Madison Square Park, 5:29 a.m.	27
TOD (Time of Death)	28
Rapes	29
This Is the Rupture of Heart	30
Apostasy	31
Hospital	32

Crematorium Limerick	33
Schweinerei	34
War	36

III. ADORED

Your Probability Amplitude	41
Letter to Lermontov	42
Live, Not Die; Live Not, Die	43
Fragment from the *Ilatease* by Homey	46
Schrödinger's Cat Is Alive	47
Bhakti (from Lord Siva to Mahadevi-Akka)	48
Love's Comely Behind	50
Raven	52
Vacana of Mahadevi-Akka to Lord Siva	53
Apple Bhagan of Mahadevi-Akka	54
Memento Mama	55
Medusa's Country	56

I

Eluded

To the Thanatos Within Me

Dear friend of ferment,
who unearths the worms

that enrich this blissful human soil,
promising the end of eternal roil:

I embrace you, dear shadow,
my revelatory friend;

dear suicidal impulse; today
I dream of the parapets above

A la Vieille Russie, and
of splattering near the Plaza

where Woody Allen wooed young girls,
leaving a bit of me

on the Strand Bookstand,
near the park and the seals—

but this is too vibrant and real.

Better to find myself alone
in a porcelain tub

with chamomile bath oil …
(as if I needed to be calm;

Larissa Shmailo

there is eternity for that),
listening to Verdi's *Requiem*,

holding a razor, or better still,
to poison myself with small

scored pills, avoiding arsenic
and the Bovary traps

of indigestion, detection;
best with caplets, red carafes

of wine or Guinness brew—
(who wouldn't want to quaff a few?)

What catharsis there is in the dive,
the gesture, the infinite jest,

the slash, the brush (its own fire),
the dance with death?

Ah, *this*: as I flirt, you draw near,
chingon to my *chingada*,

bite my ear, stop my breath—
who else could do that?

Te quiero, my Mescal, my absinthe,
my blue cyanosing corps, my Mayakovsky,

my you ...

Was this a mistake? Is it too late...?
You bite my ear, take up my rear, whisper:

Yes.

Larissa Shmailo

Gaia's Lunacy

The Sun is hot and bothered, and libidinal, having fathered
all our mendicants and tycoons, cops and robbers, and our rife
      loons.

The Earth below is verdant, child of Eros, green, exultant,
for solar love would bask her with his sure heat and not task her,

but treasure all her madmen, all her masters and their bondsmen,
thus offering a devotion of which our Gaia has no notion.

The fickle Earth presumes a love from solar powers as enough;
her denizens expect the same and bask in glory with no name.

Now, the music of the spheres should play loud in one's own ears,
but creation's power's assumed, and unheard by all us loons.

Cardiac Ghazal

My heart is sick and foul, a chest of anguished cries.
My heart attack explodes, arrest of anguished cries.

Clinicians think I'm Job; they jab and prod my veins.
Pathology requires a test of anguished cries.

They check my pulse and beats with meters stupidly.
My naked heart unrobes, undressed of anguished cries.

A sphygmomanometer can't sound my misery;
I blame my rose divine, caressed of anguished cries.

Larissa's rose is sick and is consuming me;
Cardiomyopathy, my fest of anguished cries.

Larissa Shmailo

The More You Leave

The more you leave, the more I want you back;
When you return, our love life seems to lack.
Believing you are unassailable
I yearn for you to be available.
And then you come; I cannot be more bored:
I like your leave, but not your coming toward.
Your distance charms, disarms my eager heart.
But close, I wish we were again apart.
Do stay away, and I'm forever rapt,
But now, you leave me empty, dull, and sapped.
So go away; I'll love you as before.
Love's ebb and flow is tricky as a whore.

Erasure, The Lotus Eaters, *Ulysses*[*]

BY LORRIES ALONG SIR JOHN ROGERSON'S QUAY
past Nichols' the undertaker's. Eleven, daresay.
Sent his right hand with slow grace over his hair:
Where was the chap I saw in that picture somewhere?
Ah, in the dead sea, floating on his back;
It's a law like that. Curriculum. Crack.
It's the force of gravity of the earth is the weight.
Per second, per second. Post office. Too late.
Eleven, is it? I only heard it last night.
What's wrong with him? Dead. And, he filled up, all right.
Chloroform. Laudanum. Sleeping draughts. Phlegm.
Better leave him the paper and get shut of him.

[*]Lines in this found poem are taken in order between erasures from "The Lotus Eaters" episode of *Ulysses* by James Joyce.

Larissa Shmailo

Between Eclipses[1]

A razor cuts your wrists, but
what cut you off from me?
Is true love quart'red below?

When (blew) an azure sky
separates the chambered clouds,
which Earth will you then save,
which elements recycle?

These eclipses should portend,
but I would always be
the bastard that I am,[2]
had the maidenliest, brightest star
eclipsed upon this gesture.

Fin.

---

1. It is not the grace of salvation you await, but the grace of no salvation.
2. Leer, a liar

Mean

Mediocrity, far and away, is dangerous, risk
is better than sameness.
Let the strangeness take you, whisk
mediocrity far and away. Is dangerous risk,
a Cerberus, better than tameness?
Yes, wrestling Cerberus will make you famous.
Mediocrity, far, and away! It's dangerous! Risk
is better than sameness.

Larissa Shmailo

Daddy's Elusive Love

I spent my whole life seeking it,
wrecking, reeking, eking it,
in hydra-headed phalluses;
in aliases & pal-louses;
in papapapapaMedusas;
in mirrors & seducers.

I looked for it in boxers;
in the dumps of ten detoxes;
in the roll of rundown rockers;
in anal & banal boys.

I slept with legions
in every single region;
I made love to none;
loved only one.

But it all goes back to Daddy:
Daddy, I'm your caddy;
I know you wanted a laddy;
sorry I wasn't a lady.

Family history
is largely hysterical mystery.
This old cold sold blow hold on me
is moldy genealogy.

My Vronsky

He told me, repeatedly, that
people considered him
the most intelligent person
they'd met; that he was not
more successful was a conspiracy
of minorities, lesbians, blacks, and gays,
and a coterie of cliques
that sucked up all the grants.
                      He visits me; his handsome features,
                        now marred by fat, peer at me.
                        "What are you reading?" he asks.
(A hundred pages a day, to live.)
                      He is an expert on Nabokov,
                      international relations, modern art
                      David Foster Wallace, Heidegger,
                      and the poets I translate.
(And yet he never understood *Karenina*,
any more than Nabokov did,
as they focused on the crevices
in her carriage train,
in that foreshadowed bier,
but not on the abortions,
nor the Vronsky of her death.)

Before him,
I remember feeling beautiful,
and those times people said
I was the smartest woman they knew.

Larissa Shmailo

Sunken Virgin*

A woman, I've always put them first,
denying my needs, my wants, my thirst;
Their claims pile up and pile until
I cannot walk; they importune still.
They lisp, they scream, they often stutter
I listen to the prayers they utter:
angry and frightened, cries come in tomes,
harsh and violent and hopeless poems.
I sink under the weight of their sin and hopes;
and pray for intercession from all of these dopes.

*Ekphrastic poem on a lawn Madonna sunk deeply into the earth.

The Searchers

Curled and inert, an El Greco Christ:
death has pulled your form so long, forlorn.
What church father said we were *urinum* and feces,
urinum, sputum, and phlegm?
As if these last moments of wet last release,
the bloody catheter and the mucous lung,
could take from me, my bicameral mind,
with a chamber owned solely by you;
with a net of live neurons, a billion or more
imprinted on your face alone,
take the sight of you, bending, tall at the door,
smiling and coming home;
or the memory of your strong arms, young and hard,
lifting me up when I fell,
as John Wayne in *The Searchers* lifted Natalie Wood,
when a nail pierced my foot through my shoe.
As rusty we became, as foreign to each other,
till this parting, in your arms, in this embrace. *Proschai.*

II

Deluded

My Dead

My husband lost his shirt at cards; insolvent, he then drowned
in slick Cancun on our honeymoon; years now, it still astounds
how fast, how fast, a living hell can turn a life around.

My godchild told me pointedly if she were to attempt
to die that she'd succeed at once; her word she quickly kept,
and took a hundred opiates and drifted to her death.

My punk-rock pimp, a crush of mine, loved theater and art.
He sodomized and strangled a young man close to his heart,
then packed a bag of bondage toys and left for foreign parts.

Before her death, my mother called and calmly sat me down;
if she could do it all again, she'd have no children, none.
She lived her life in anger and, despite us, all alone.

My father drank and slept around; he was a well-liked guy.
He said *I love you* once to me the night before he died.
Was there a feeling come too late or panic in his eyes?

Larissa Shmailo

He Called Me "Fat"

He called me "fat," and I cringed, not
at the insult, as such (not much of one)
but at the verbal dull, the paucity of
adjective, the pervading mental lull, the
flap of his limp and flaccid gums, the lack of
hearty fun. Fat? Why *fat*, I cried? Surely,
round would move things up a pitch or two,
and *gargantuan* would do, and *corpulent*
construe the adipose goo at hand. Why *fat*, oh,
fatuous man? Call me *beefy, blimp*, or *bulging*;
term me *bovine, bull*, or *burly*; name me *chunky,
roly-poly*, or inflated as your nog. O linguini,
limp and little! Your linguistic torpor bores, ignores
the 25,000 words that Joyce and Shakespeare
forged, and do not hoard (but your words,
overall, are snores). As I eat my s'mores,
let's resume: I am *thickset, paunchy, heavy*
as the synapses in you; I am wider than a
canyon and the broad primordial stew. Fat?
Fat, you fraud? I am Queen of unburnt calorie,
the rarest elephantine; the Mobyest of
sentient beasts; the diet doctor's dream.
My stockiness drives diet stock, my pudge
the script of pills; I am larger than Niagara
and the Roman seven hills. Dormant doormat,
there are spas of verdant bliss for me, but no
school for fools like you. You are but a speck of
rotten lard, a granule of mere sand; I am high and
vast and infinite, dimensionally great and grand.

Heart Murmur

A murmured heart, with nature's slow hand beating,
is mine, dear master-monster of my passion;
no woman's feeble heart, but not revealing
itself to you, afraid of your rejection.
I fear no scythe that swiftly cuts all deeds down
that mocks bold love, loud fame, and futile wealth
than death of words I hope in heart you might own,
the syllables I cherish, prayed in stealth.
Your eye is false, blue-bright, my own Narcissus;
your words dissemble even as they call;
your heart beats not for me nor other mistress;
your empty heart can't know love's blood at all.
You'll be my heart, a numb, reflexive pleasure
to beat, half-heart, and never know full flexure.

Larissa Shmailo

The Trick Wants to Go to Plato's

My trick wants to go to Plato's.
We go to the old Ansonia Baths
where a thousand gay men fucked
a thousand times a night for years.

Now it is Plato's Retreat; no single men
are allowed without a date.
I sign a document attesting that I am
not a prostitute; my whore name is Nora,

after Ibsen; I add Nader, going green for Ralph,
and strip. I scarf down a bagel, hard and cold,
at the buffet, look in the angled light at the rich
naked people, some still shyly wearing their towels,

and dive:
I go into the mattress room.

A daisy chain has formed, a length of copulating people,
each one on the left servicing the right, up and down.
The trick is suddenly timid and urges me to start:
He will watch. There is cunnilingus to the middle-aged blonde

then a line of men; they find me and move in, one by one,
young, old, some good looking, most average at best.
We fuck. And fuck. And fuck again.
Suddenly comes a man, hirsute, pressing, he disgusts me.

I push him away and he pushes back hard,
but on the chain beside me, a languid man
turns to him and says, Sir, the lady said no, and miraculously,
the ape disappears. I feel a moment of gratitude,

extinguished by the semen of the next man.

I work every day. After three tricks,
I wait for my pimp at midnight at the door of
Studio 54; he falls out of a cab in sneakers and tie,
carrying his poetry notebooks and a book by

Roland Barthes. Steve Rubell himself lets us in.
I follow the pimp to the floor and we dance; he dances well.
He is like the bottles of cheap amyl nitrate he carries for sex,
    dizzying, sickening, my freebase, my cocaine.

The manager for my house, Friends with Style,
is a small misshapen man with an ugly face;
He tells me he went to Yale.
I work the phones and the tricks come in.

First the Hassid, and this *shiksa* was his practice.
Harry Abram's son brings me a book of Magritte.
Sarah and I do a three-way with a red-haired man
who says he knows Reggie Jackson; of course we are impressed.

Later in the day, when it is quiet and
I am alone, a cop comes in; I freeze; I know he is insane.

Larissa Shmailo

He says *are you going to be nice to me, girl?*
He puts my hand on his crotch and I

feel the metal of his gun and he grins and says,
Baby, if you are going to flirt with death,
you are going to get a date.

A man rescues me from the life. In Cuernavaca
I climb the volcanoes every day and heal.
Unable to understand human kindness
I leave him and go back to New York.

Two years pass, I am in trouble again.
I need 200 bucks, the house where I worked is
a sex club now. Drunk off my ass, I do a man and
his wife in the bathtub, then a pair of rutting men .

Standing by the fireplace, I see a girl there,
blonde, pale, underage; I see she has cut herself up
and down her slender arms and I, the fucking role model,
beg her to go home, and she only laughs bitterly.

A thug from the Ray's Pizza next door sees us talking
and tells me,
Mix it up, get back to work
and I become angry, enraged, I go beserk:

I turn on him:
I am going to tear this punk's balls off with my hands

if he touches this little girl.
And I get into his flat punk face and say:

WHAT THE FUCK MORE DO YOU WANT?
and then I black out.

When I come to, a big Irishman
is throwing me down two flights of stairs.
I land on the concrete on 76th and Third;
stone-cold sober now; I feel no pain.

I call the police and they come; the old one is coarse;
the young one tells me that he has gone to college and read books.
They will not bust the house. I curse them for ball-less wimps.
They say *Go home, miss, go home,*

and I end up in Bellevue, old Bellevue, locked ward
where four orderlies, four, have to hold me down to shoot
      Thorazine up my butt,
and I am put in four-point restraint.

My new shrink, hired by my sister,
comes in on a Sunday from Connecticut.
He brings me a carton of Benson and Hedges
cigarettes and says, "These are like gold in here."
They are.

Bellevue, Bellevue, where the nurses' crazy laughter
rings high through the night,

Larissa Shmailo

where *boriquenas pequenas* cry *mamí, mamí da me un peso.*
I think they say *beso.*

Soon, the DTs start, and I shake uncontrollably.
A homeless man, thin, dirty, tall,
puts his veteran's jacket 'round my shoulders and disappears,
a Quixote to my Aldonza in this wretched place.

Madison Square Park, 5:29 a.m.

Dawn: I wake in the park, face puffy and red;
Liquid, brown tallboys, broken glass, at my head.
The bench is cool, my shoes are gone, my fishnet stockings torn;
I wish I were elsewhere, lived differently, was safe or never born.

Policemen tell me, broke and blackly bruised, to move along;
I find cardboard in the garbage, make a sign, sing a song.
A teenager stops, sings with me, and blushing. averts his eyes;
Women pass, scorn me, prouder than they'd be otherwise.

A businessman winks, gives nothing; a serviceman gives a buck.
Men hang out windows; one screams obscenities from his truck.
What some men will hit on, eagerly, still astonishes me;
You are never too sick, too dirty, or too old, apparently.

Larissa Shmailo

TOD (Time of Death)

All ways blocked, and future gloomy; suicide seems bright and
    roomy;
Now's my chance for rebirth, I will leave this dismal life role.
I'll return as Queen of Sheba, or a vampire, or a reiver,
or a saint who cures the *nouveaux riches*, a wondrous, wealthy soul.
Yes, you see, I've found my niche, to preach and prosper,
    marvelous goal!
(Pills I took just took their toll.)

Now I feel my limbs start numbing; still, my brain is bright and
    humming:
Opiates *are* worth exploration, Percocet's a true vacation.
Who's afraid of drug addiction? Warning labels purport fiction.
Strange, my blood's slow circulation—what's up with my
    respiration?
Is this *my* Death's anticipation? Death now or imagination?
Death's approach now, or elation?

As my last act I will vomit, weakened, I will choke upon it.
As it turns out, life is real; and death the realest part; I depart.
While I thought of death as drama, it became this final trauma:
Painful ebbing consciousness, in shit and urine, and this last fart.
Life continues always, right? Now stop this, God, let's just
    restart …
(Cause of death, attack by heart.)

Rapes

I abandoned myself to invisible hands,
the known vice and strong vise of my nerves and my glands.
I half-screwed and cat-moaned and imagined your stare
in the stranger, his knife slowly teasing my hair.[1]

I abandoned myself to invisible hands,
to old limerence[2], feminine amorous trance,
and I censured myself: "You're hysterical." Him,
and the rape became me, now a phantom sex limb.

I abandoned myself to invisible hands
and faced memory, resentment, and fear, and command.[3]
Why were you just like him? Why so many to fear?[4]
This old lead lives in me, this tar asphalt of tears.[5]

---

1. A bandit took my breathing;
    A date rape! howled the frat;
    A roofie took the edge off;
    The rapist called me fat.
2. An obsessive romantic infatuation, usually unrequited and/or inappropriate and painful.
3. Through the ability to understand how little you cared, I grew strong. I forgave and forgot you, like used toilet paper, flushed.
4. I knew, knew what you were when I chose you. The rapist not so much, but you, my voluntary rape. Because I believed you when you said this is what I deserved. Because I helped you break my spirit and soil my dreams.
5. I am now 100 percent responsible for my life, and no pain can take that away from me.

Larissa Shmailo

This Is the Rupture of Heart

This is the rupture of heart; love's sharp scalpel will cut mine apart.
Only a surgeon could see how to operate so well on me.
This is the intricate pain, come dissecting my frog hurt again.
Eros is clinically bold, and a professional, totally cold.

Apostasy

There is a God; there is none but me.
Doubt tortures me, lying like a whore.
Still I pray daily, but I'm mad, you see.

My bond with God, since I am crazy,
Is special; why else would I suffer for?
There is a God; there is none but me.

Am I divine, theologically free?
And no other God, and nothing more?
Still I pray daily, but I'm mad, you see.

The *zazen* moment gazing at the sea:
There must be something more to adore.
There is a God; there is none but me.

After torture and rape a child dies, finally;
The suffering of innocents, God's gaping sore.
Still I pray daily, but I'm mad, you see.

If God is God, is God good, truly?
Can The Christ now rise, settle this score?
There is a God; there is none but me.
Still I pray daily, but I'm mad, you see.

Larissa Shmailo

Hospital

Jaded and exhausted nurses walk the wards
repeating curses; dying patients call for mother,
crying for a glass of water. Greedy doctors
buy stock options, sell us meds containing toxins;
leeches would be more effective than these MDs'
best directives. People tired and sick, emergent,
can't get help though help is urgent. Here a man is
screaming, bleeding, here a woman's life's receding.
Richer folk may think they're served well, wind up
in the same prescribed hell. Hear me, patients, for
your welfare, this is not the place for healthcare.

Crematorium Limerick

My mother said (dear, dearest Mum)
In camp Dora was no crematorium.
Then, she said that there was, so,
As a guard there she would know;
But truth-telling just hurt her poor tum.

Larissa Shmailo

Schweinerei

Get up, schweinerei, *my father says, waking us late*
And at dinner, my dyadya, *talking drunk and loud,*
says that he and my dedushka *guarded railroads*
for the Germans in the war. The railroads are old,

but this country is new: not the Soviet Union, I ask?,
not wanting to know. Barely breathing: the world,
hard, atrocious, and cruel, falls into place.
And Babushka? *Babushka worked at the railroad, too.*

(I feel her hard hands braiding my hair, the stern
lips mouthing: zhid*). I remember my mother, seeking*
salvation at her grave, saying: "I once opened a gate."
The world falls into place. What was on those rails?

Who?

And what did their guards do?

Somehow I knew, I always knew.

Tonight, I hear my mother's reedy voice simper, singing,
Auf jeden Dezember folgt wieder ein Mai. *Her home of*
gemutlichkeit, *comfort without joy. Her love for the*

German tongue; how often she said "There were good
Germans, too." As Ukrainians, save the martyred few,
they were gvardia, kapos, *collaborators, too. Did they have*
a choice? Starvation in the kolkhoz, *bodies lying, dying*

*in the streets, and only the Germans, said my mother,
protested Stalin's rape and collectivization of the
Ukraine. How much victim? How much volunteer?*

*In Kalinivka, the mass graves; my family was there.
In Prymsl, deported Jews; my family was there.
In Erfurt where crematoria were made, my family was there.
In the Harz Mountains, Northhausen and Dora-Mittelbau; too.*

What other families? Who survived, and why?

*In the face of starvation, of death, of Stalin's camps,
tell me, you, well-fed and safe, judging me and mine: is there
complicity when there is no choice? (Was there choice?)*

*The stories, the lacunae, the lies. Now I know why I always felt
like a Jew. O, Adonai, why? Why these origins for me, why no
orisons for me? The dead are dead, but not within me, my
holocaust today, forever my bread.*

Larissa Shmailo

War

> For C.K. Williams

I.

Reading the prose of young media scribes, absorbed, as they are, with sex and money, and the need for status, even among orgiasts, I pause. How they claw, struggling for cabs, cars with bars, and the nod from Cerberus at the door of the club, as if from him, his acceptance, could come entrée to it all, the whole nine circles of desire. But Buddha was right, and it makes for lousy verse, the cascade to the fallen from fulfilled. The rituals are old, and the same rachitic claw reaches over us all. And so, torn, we tear, primordial as the air.

II.

We live in parts. The rich ones know. Their eyes caress metals, held tightly to the chest, played closely to the vest, thrown stingily among the just-good-folks. You won't find the address of an arms factory anywhere. *We don't know.* An igniter built in Chappaqua, a pull-pin glazed in Maine, in Idaho a shell. We need arms, military muscle, American dough. *Watch it blow.*

Skeleton, skeleton, step on a crack,
live grenade payback, Jack Iraq.
Shrapnel tears run moist and red.
There, there, there, there (he was six)
there, there, there, there (she has no hand)
there, there, there (his spine is torn)
there, there, there (her head is gone).

III.

A small time to be alive. A very small time to be alive, short enough to pretend we've done no harm. Thanatos is a blind-man's bluff, an ignoramus with a stake, a what-were-we-thinking?, a mistake.

How did we not know there was really no other? How could we, eyes and legs, mouths and heart, all the same, damn it, same, how could we see anything else but we? No fires or fall, just beloved all?

Maybe as the last breath—will we know it as last?— as the last breath goes, we—will we know any we?—we might feel another's dying breath that we might know someone else's as we know our own death.

III

Adored

Your Probability Amplitude

I glance and
a boson blinks
into view.

A strong force
beckons

even as
a weak force
radios decay.

The gravity
of the situation

the magnetism:

I observe and
my attention

turns particles into power
tracks into trails
whims into waves.

Larissa Shmailo

Letter to Lermontov

You are distant, alone, and far on the horizon,
obscured, almost nurtured, by the ocean's fog.
Seeking and searching, you are always a stranger:
What did leaving me, losing me, cost?

I would swim with one foot on the sand of the dry land;
I would wait for you, never explore.
But you are the waves, and the wind and its whistle,
and the storm you embrace far from shore.

My few timid ships all cling to the shoreline,
too frightened to leave what they know.
You laugh and command them: There is another shore;
the second appears when the first is gone.

So sing, my dear love, of the wide morning's gold sky,
and the call of the azure strand,
and the gull and the salt and the mast that pitches,
and the lure of a foreign land.

I will be your welcome, your country forever;
I'll receive, then release you (adieu).
I will be your native and nurturing homeland
and wait to be called home by you.

Live, Not Die: Live Not, Die

Now, how shall it continue, bright primate? How shall this be punctuated? An Oxfordian series, cursive, moving ever on, entailing every monkey, all keyboards in existence, black and white, and all of Shakespeare's work? Therein lies a tail. Is my silly, hoping life, then, the parentheses in the mind of a savage, loving god, or a twitching, rapid question in the tick-tock of the void? Comma or coma? Which is it to be? Angels,

you decide. Faster: My hope today, a ferocious, hankering monkey, wrestles with Thanatos in my psyche's mud, a bout observed by angels, and, truly, always about you; my demons, who intone Shakespeare's verse like a Polonius behind a curtain, his platitudes punctuated by doubt, growing like a semicolon in my gut, close these parentheses without fortitude or Fortinbras, a Hamlet dangling on his question.

Larissa Shmailo

Come, ask me if I dare, beloved, before I go, to ask the question: Would you say, turning me aside, as an afterthought, in parentheses, "That is not what I meant at all," leaving me, a grinning, groping monkey, to chase distant mermaids in the sea spray, those soggy singing angels who sing to drowning women like me? I am not brave, not Shakespeare's heroine, and will not declaim mercy for men in a speech punctuated

by all wisdom, warm, maternal, eternal, I am, rather, a rattled, tangled monkey, fur matted, teeth sharp, staring down my death in a showdown punctuated by words, words, words, words, words, words; and those in parentheses whisper with epithets of my end; here I sit, periodic, asking the angels, how long a sentence I will have, and will I ever write one as good as Shakespeare's? "Two bees, and not two bees, and they're soon extinct, too"; begging the question,

petitio principii: assuming the initial point, how shall I get to the final, punctuated by logical fallacies, tautologies, circular, as raw as the tail ass of a monkey; me, to persuade you, had we words enough for time, there could be no question, no crime, in assuming infinity, in basking in eternity like seraphim, bright angels whose divine lust could last a trillion biers and years, through a million Shakespeares' lines; but our lives are slashed by a Ginzo knife through the tail, trapped in parentheses.

To the period's point now, signaled by a capital flourish and punctuated with the Oxfordian serial clause (I should have been a pair of claws instead of monkey balls): given infinity, when my molecules scatter, on some infinite star populated by angels, might they not reassemble as me, my primate self, with you, a man as fine as Shakespeare's best, again, to dance together, coupled, contained in divine parentheses)? For the thought of you, whom I love, I trouble the divine to ask this question.

My monkey question is not eloquent, nor metaphysical as angels:
It stands in parentheses, rolls not from the tongue as Shakespeare's,
but loves you, period, whichever is punctuated, in eternity or extinction.

Larissa Shmailo

Fragment from the *Ilatease* of Homey, from a Recently Discovered Mycenaean Text

… Cythera of the white and widening arse who stalked strong Lactid on the Bluvian Isles; ah, strong-latted Lactid, of the swaying sword whose droop in battle was legend from the Bluvias to the Effluvias to the damp and puddly Lluvias; a legend, god-written, of Elera smitten (to whit, her Attic tits), clad of Hephaestus's mittens.
Ah, Bluvias, where the gold and green and pink and silver and ivory and indigo and carmine and slightly beige-ish-off-mauve-ish fishes fall to the net and the bent, spent trident of Poseidon, who, green-maned, sea-stained, and a tad weight-gained, also wore Hephaestus's mittens as he made love to Cythera, who looked a bit like Elera, except fatter in the arse.
How unlike Myrcon the Dorkan, unmittened and unbitten, on the shores of Elephantinosis, where the nasty biting ponies play in spent, bent Poseidon's spray … .
(Here the fragment of the *Ilatease* ends.)

Tr. L. Shmailo

Schrödinger's Cat Is Alive

MRI won't be till Thursday;
waiting is a practiced sense;
anyone can face life's dangers—
takes the strong to bear suspense.

MRI with contrast or not,
little magnets map the brain.
Soon I'll feel my body changing,
entering another plane.

All I am is quarks and gluons,
energy and impulse-filled;
There is no material realm here,
and these quanta can't be killed.

So I wait without much straining;
courage comes from quanta, too.
I'm the field of every being;
parts of me are parts of you.

Don't look toward a grave to see me;
my old soul has other plans;
All of me will dance with helium,
I'll be sun, and leaves, and grass.

Larissa Shmailo

Bhakti (from Lord Siva to Mahadevi-Akka)

It is in the experience of the ignorant that we learn:
When you have learned, I will destroy
all those who hurt you
and their thoughts within you;
both the lords of your rebirth, and the master whores
who took your night's wages from you.
I will feed these wolf children woe, words, and wealth:
Endless, they will talk until they choke.

For them that hurt you
I will give claws to walk on,
dirt beneath the nails that bury
lies beneath their feet.

And you will be my body, never-returning,
remembered as temple and body alone.
And you will be my lotus, ever-returning,
remembered as body, my temple alone.

The beat of my rhythm be the pulse of your song,
my meter, your timbral and gong.
The poem to destroy your illusions is written
by Lord Siva's true Bhakti's tongue.

Come choose, my beloved, the good dharma or ill:
My lightning and thunder will strike where you will.
When the road rises weary and the wolves find you faint,
I will strew it with holy men, teachers, and saints
that ignorance may tickle your toes.

And you will be my body, never-returning,
remembered as temple and body alone.
And you will be my lotus, ever-returning,
remembered as body, my temple alone.

You will leave your wise men:
Your mind, with no object to rest on,
will ride on the horse of my breath;
I will make love to you between rebirths
with penis and womb, with land and sea,
with wind and sun and death.

And you will be my body, never-returning,
Remembered as temple and body alone.
And you will be my lotus, ever-returning,
Remembered as body and temple alone.

And if you miss salvation, never-returning,
I will offer it, Bhakti, ever-returning,
again and again and again.

Larissa Shmailo

Love's Comely Behind

Say, is not all love illicit and blind?
True, it hides, undone, in the mind.

*Who knows Allah's thoughts truly loves
the Self that is Allah's own wisdom to know,
and you are Allah's, my milk, sheep, and doves,
unsure yet certain, a dervish in the snow.*

Did you, today, attend upon love?
No, intent instead, you will not find.

*Who knows Allah's thoughts truly loves
the Self that is Allah's own wisdom to know,
and you are Allah's, my milk, sheep, and doves,
unsure yet certain, a dervish in the snow.*

Greedily, you eat and fruit is gone.
Pulp devoured, you hold the rind.

*Who knows Allah's thoughts truly loves
the Self that is Allah's own wisdom to know,
and you are Allah's, my milk, sheep, and doves,
unsure yet certain, a dervish in the snow.*

You have lost your love? O, sing, fool:
Now gaze upon love's comely behind.

*Who knows Allah's thoughts truly loves
the Self that is Allah's own wisdom to know,*

and you are Allah's, my milk, sheep, and doves,
unsure yet certain, a dervish in the snow.

I love love's desert and its snow.
I, Shmailo, dervish, a lover signed.

Larissa Shmailo

Raven

She will tread on the stones near the sea,
On the red and blood stones by the sea.
She will answer the call of the gulls;
She will cry raven words just to me.
I will answer her cry with a screech;
I will offer my gull's heart to her:
To her raven and raptor-black eyes,
To her torn, ribboned-red, precious feet.

Vacana of Mahadevi-Akka to Lord Siva

Nataraja, white as jasmine, fill me.
Lord, hair matted from love, still me.
Indra Deva of the meeting rivers, kill me.
Let eight hundred forty thousand hard deaths take me,
As you, Bhadra-Bhima, won't forsake me.
Laugh, brother Blue Throat, for the poison we will drink.
Brother-lover-husband-son, I'll sing and will not think.
Shakra, Lord Asura, take the burden of my tears.
Now, Indra Deva, take the tribute of my years.

Larissa Shmailo

Apple Bhagan of Mahadevi-Akka

When death comes, it will be diamond-white.
The dark months before, a falling, burying brown.
All is, after all, a trap of activity,
before
the bursting scent, naked, of apples gone ground.

When death comes, it will be sister's hand,
as callused as ground, the slapping of time.
It is, after all, the root of activity,
so like
the dusted brown bottles of sour apple wine.

When death comes, it will be clear and bright.
All actions, after all, from ignorance arise,
The cycle of rebirth will dance with Lord Siva
becoming
as babies like apples, born breathing, born red.

Memento Mama

I haven't passed that dream of wisdom,
the borders you crossed through.

I can't translate the language
I thought I thought I knew.

I see a meaning, watching you die,
hold it in my hands like a graying sigh,

this lock of hair which I comb and tie.
I kiss the head which hears my no,

and meet your eyes, and say: Don't go.
and leave you to this tongue of dread:

This is me, it cries, this is me and I die.
We will all speak these words in this way
and then, and till then, what shall I say?

Larissa Shmailo

Medusa's Country

I had come to your house in your cave of trees
To face you like the rain.
My frozen limbs moved, my arm ready to touch
You, my reflection, in pain.

When your rheumy eyes were before me
Your once ash-blonde hair
Your stiff limbs reached out, like serpents
With skin shed everywhere.

This I acknowledge begrudgingly:
Nothing is always young.
My own cave will not brighten nor bless nor confer
Joy on any man's tongue.

The water will dry and will leave only dust;
I will feel no prick when it does.
The serpentine grass will cover my love
And green growth enshroud what was.

But once a man stood like a statue
Before my cave of trees
His eyes transfixed by my serpents
That hardened, froze, and pleased.

Acknowledgments

Poems in *Medusa's Country* have appeared in the following journals:

The Common Online: "*Schweinerei*"

Cryopoetry: "Sestina: Live, Not Die; Live Not, Die"

The Enchanting Verses Literary Review: "Love's Comely Behind"

Exquisite Duet, JMWW: "Rapes"

FULCRUM: "Between Eclipses," "Erasure, The Lotus Eaters, *Ulysses*," "He Called Me Fat," "Letter to Lermontov," "Vacana of Mahadevi-Akka to Lord Siva"

Journal of Feminist Studies in Religion: "Apple Bhagan of Mahadevi-Akka"

Journal of Poetics Research: "Gaia's Lunacy"

Levure littéraire: "To the Thanatos Within Me," "War"

New Mirage Journal: "Daddy's Elusive Love," "Memento Mama"

Plume: "Your Probability Amplitude," "Fragment from the *Ilatease* of Homey, from a Recently Discovered Mycenaean Text"

Sensitive Skin: "Erasure, The Lotus Eaters, *Ulysses*"

The St. Petersburg Review: "My Vronsky," "The Searchers"

Unlikely Stories Mark V: " The Trick Wants to Go to Plato's," "Bhakti," "TOD (Time of Death)," "Sunken Virgin"

"*Verde Que Te Quiero Verde*": *Poems after Federico Garcia Lorca*, ed. Natalie Peeterse, Second Edition, Open Country Press: "To the Thanatos Within Me"

About the Author

LARISSA SHMAILO's work appears in *Measure for Measure* (Everyman's Library/Penguin Random House), *Words for the Wedding* (Perigee/Penguin Putnam), and *Contemporary Russian Poetry* (Dalkey Archive Press). Larissa's other poetry collections are *#specialcharacters* (Unlikely Books), *In Paran* (BlazeVOX [books]), and the chapbooks *A Cure for Suicide* (Červená Barva Press), and *Fib Sequence* (Argotist Ebooks). Her poetry CDs are *The No-Net World* and *Exorcism* (SongCrew); tracks are available from Spotify, iTunes, Deezer, Muze, and Amazon. Her novel *Patient Women* is available from Amazon, BN.com, and BlazeVOX [books].

Larissa is editor-in-chief of the anthology *Twenty-first Century Russian Poetry* (Big Bridge Press). She translated *Victory over the Sun* for the Los Angeles County Museum of Art's celebrated reconstruction of the first Futurist opera; the libretto has been used for productions at Brooklyn Academy of Music, the Smithsonian, Boston University, and the Garage Museum of Moscow. She also has been a translator on the Russian Bible for the Eugene A. Nida Institute for Biblical Scholarship of the American Bible Society.

Larissa's work is archived at the Museum of Modern Art (MoMA), the Los Angeles County Museum of Art, the Hirsshorn Museum of the Smithsonian, and seven universities. She was a finalist in the Glass Woman prose prize in 2012, and a semifinalist in the Subito Press/ University of Boulder prose competition in 2014. Larissa received the New Century Music awards for best spoken word with rock, jazz, and electronica in 2009, as well as the best album award for *Exorcism*. She has read at the Knitting Factory, Barnard College, the New School, New York University, the Langston Hughes residence, and for American Express/Share Our Strength. She blogs at http://larissashmailo.blogspot.com/ Please see Larissa's Wikipedia page and website at www.larissashmailo.com.

www.ingramcontent.com/pod-product-compliance
Lightning Source LLC
LaVergne TN
LVHW011430080426
835512LV00005B/361